In Session

Carlos Santana

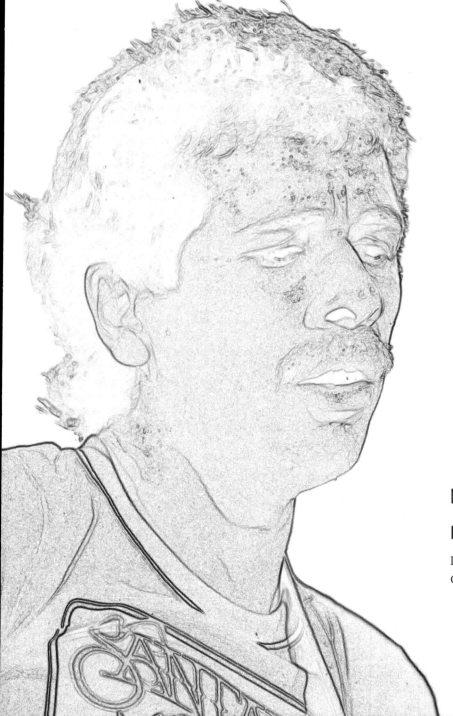

International Music Publications Limited

Griffin House, 161 Hammersmith Road, London W6 8BS

DON'T BE A MUSIC COPYCAT!

The copying of © copyright material is a criminal offence and may lead to prosecution.

Series Editor: Sadie Cook

Music transcription, arrangement and recording: Martin Shellard
Music Editorial & Project Management: Artemis Music Limited
Cover Photo by Max Redfern,
All photos supplied by Redferns Music Picture Library
Design & Production: Space DPS Limited
Reproduced and printed by Halstan & Co. Ltd., Amersham, Bucks., England

Published 1999

© International Music Publications Limited
Griffin House, 161 Hammersmith Road, London W6 8BS

Exclusive Distributors:

International Music Publications Limited

England: Griffin House
161 Hammersmith Road
London W6 8BS

Germany: Marstallstr. 8
D-80539 München

Denmark: Danmusik
Vognmagergade 7
DK1120 Copenhagen K

Italy: Via Campania 12
20098 San Giuliano Milanese
Milano

Spain: Magallanes 25
28015 Madrid

France: 29 Rue de la Ville-l'Eveque
75008 Paris

WARNER BROS. PUBLICATIONS U.S. INC.

USA: 15800 N.W. 48th Avenue
Miami, Florida 33014

Australia: 3 Talavera Road
North Ryde
New South Wales 2113

Scandinavia: P.O. Box 533
Vendevagen 85 B
S-182 15 Danderyd
Sweden

In Session with

Carlos Santana

In the Book...

On The CD...

Biography

Growing up in Tijuana, Mexico in the 1950s, Carlos Santana was introduced to music by his father, Jose, a mariachi violinist. At the tender age of eight, young Carlos caught the guitar playing bug, and began emulating the styles of such blues greats as B.B. King, John Lee Hooker and T-Bone Walker. He began playing in various bands on the 'Tijuana Strip', and it was during this formative period that the seeds of his unique guitar playing style were sown.

In 1960 Carlos' family moved to San Francisco, where he enthusiastically immersed himself in that city's melting pot of a musical culture. For the next five years Carlos continued to develop his blend of blues, rock and roll, and his native Mexican music.

In 1966 he joined forces with Gregg Rolie to form the Santana Blues Band, which became a popular group on the San Francisco blues scene. In 1969, with the band's name shortened to Santana they were launched into the public eye with a legendary performance at that year's Woodstock festival in front of 500,000 people. It was the era of flower power, love was in the air, and Santana had arrived. The distinctive musical elements of Afro-Caribbean percussion and Carlos' soulful guitar playing combined in a unique blend, creating a powerful musical identity that would launch the band to stardom.

Their debut album SANTANA was released in that same year, and went platinum. It contained the now classic tracks *Evil Ways* and *Soul Sacrifice*, and the follow-up album ABRAXAS included *Black Magic Woman* and *Samba Pa Ti*. After the third album SANTANA III they released an album that was to mark a definite change in style. For openers there was a personnel change – Carlos enlisted the skills of a young guitarist called Neal Schon who would later go on to form Journey with Gregg Rolie. More importantly, this was about the time when Carlos began to follow the teachings of spiritual guru Sri Chinmoy, taking the additional name Devadip, meaning 'Light Of The Lamp Supreme'. This change was reflected in his music, which also seemed to take on a new persona. Songs such as *Song Of The Wind* and the album LOVE DEVOTION AND SURRENDER, which was recorded with fellow Sri Chinmoy devotee John McLaughlin, are much more abstract and improvisational, allowing Carlos to demonstrate the full range of his expressive style.

> " *...the momentum he's built up by gradually increasing his speed finally catapults him up to a higher level...* "

Photo: David Re

Photo: Ebet Roberts

> ❝...*showcases Santana's dynamic and lyrical style, he uses the volume control to change the volume and tone of the guitar.* ❞

The next five years saw the release of many classic Santana albums including WELCOME, BORBOLETTO, FESTIVAL and MOONFLOWER which contained a cover of The Zombies' *She's Not There,* Santana's biggest ever UK hit.

The MARATHON and ZEBOP! albums of 1979 and 1981 showed a more commercial rock edge, though still coloured with driving Latin percussion. The late eighties and nineties saw Santana return to their musical roots with albums like VIVA SANTANA and MILAGRO, which is dedicated to the memories of Miles Davis and Bill Graham.

An extremely prolific artist, Carlos has released over thirty titles and sold over thirty million albums since 1969 including collaborations with such jazz luminaries as Wayne Shorter, Herbie Hancock and Buddy Miles.

Musical Style

Carlos has a unique and distinctive style, partly due to his Latin American background, which finds its way into all aspects of his playing. His trademark sustained, crying guitar sound came from his stated desire to 'sing' with his guitar, always trying to emulate the vocal qualities of singers like soul legend Aretha Franklin. This search for sustain and tone has lead to many significant developments in guitar equipment. He was one of the first people to use Mesa Boogie amplifiers and Paul Reed Smith guitars, and he had a hand in the design of the Yamaha SG 2000 guitar. His sound is loud but never shrill, and when he plays he says that he uses his whole body, not just his hands, to *project* the notes.

That famous endless sustain is achieved by finding a 'sweet spot' between himself and his amplifier, with some of the top rolled off, which allows the guitar to feed back in a controlled and musical way.

The key to understanding Carlos' guitar style is to study the detail in his phrasing. His use of staccato notes and decorations in lyrical lines lends immense musicality to his playing and, unusually for a guitarist, his use of vibrato is very sparse and subtle. These are all elements that we'll look at in detail later in the book.

Performance Notes

Flor D'Luna

Taken from the 1977 album MOONFLOWER this track is a mid tempo instrumental with a strong samba flavour. It's in the key of D minor but you'll notice that Carlos doesn't stick to the standard pentatonic position for the melody. These position changes are an important part of the melody as he uses the different sound of each string to complement the musical phrases.

The solo is based on the Em7♭5, A7, Dm chord sequence. This is called a II V I progression and is very common in jazz. The solo is based mainly around the

10th fret D minor pentatonic scale. Notice how the energy level increases firstly by him playing faster and faster phrases then, later, by changing position and playing in a higher register. It's as if the momentum he's built up by gradually increasing his speed finally catapults him up to a higher level. This is a great example of solo building technique by one of the acknowledged masters.

Notice how the outro uses the same chord progression as the solo with Carlos ad-libbing to the end.

All I Ever Wanted

This is an up-tempo riff-based rock number from the 1979 album MARATHON. The piece starts with a distinctive two bar percussion intro before the guitar plays an opening E major riff, leading to the first verse.

The rhythm guitar drops out here and a bluesy lead guitar loosely follows the vocal line based around the E major pentatonic scale (E, G♯, A, B, C♯, E). A new riff leads into and accompanies the second verse before we see yet another change of texture with the power chords in the chorus. This is a great example of arranging – notice how the various sections are treated differently to help point up the form of the song.

In contrast to the high energy riffs, the solo is quite restrained with Carlos leaving space to allow the solo to 'breathe' preferring to use simple, repetitive ideas rather than overloading the song with notes.

Carlos leaves space to allow the solo to 'breathe'

Hannibal

This is a high energy, Latin instrumental from the ZEBOP! album and features some of Santana's most incendiary guitar playing. Although the key is G minor, the tune is based around a D minor tonality which gives it an exotic, modal flavour.

The opening of the song features a Spanish style nylon-string acoustic over a power chord backing, setting the tone for the distorted lead guitar melody.

The main melody is split into two sections, the first played at the 5th fret position and the second around the 10th. The second section is much looser than the first with more fills and position shifts.

When the chanted vocal comes in the guitar plays a palm-muted riff in unison with the bass and piano which leads into a percussion break. This percussion break is punctuated by a unison figure at the beginning of each bar, creating a dramatic framework for the improvised percussion.

The energy is kept at maximum throughout the solo, from the opening fast-picked scales to the double string bends and syncopated chords at the end.

> *"...the energy is kept at maximum throughout the solo..."*

SANTANAdiscography

Photo: Robert Knight

Sensitive Kind

Another track from the ZEBOP! album, this is a laid-back vocal ballad originally written and recorded by J J Cale. The key is G minor and most of the guitar action takes place at either the 3rd fret position or an octave higher at the 15th fret. Check out Carlos' usual range of articulations here, and how he cleverly contrasts staccato notes with more lyrical bends and slurs. This is a common feature in all his music – it's part of his musical 'fingerprint'.

The solo is another example of restraint and economical playing. Notice how the simple yet soulful phrases are punctuated by rests. Once again the energy level of this solo increases towards the end, with Carlos both playing more notes and moving to a higher register.

Samba Pa Ti

Originally from the album ABRAXAS, this slow, melodic ballad showcases Santana's dynamic and lyrical style. He uses the volume control throughout to change both the volume and tone of the guitar. Listen carefully and you can hear that almost every phrase has a slightly different tone, with some phrases so quiet they are almost inaudible. Although this song is in the key of G the main melody is played around the 5th fret A minor position.

The beat moves into double time for the solo which starts with a melodic idea taken from the previous section. This then expands into a long free-ranging solo as Santana stretches out over the G to Am7 chord sequence. As in most of Santana's songs the solo is played over a simple two or three chord backing which allows him the freedom to express himself without being tied down to a restrictive chord progression.

Europa

This track is another melodic ballad, this time played over a jazz-inspired chord sequence. First released on the 1977 album MOONFLOWER, it features not only Santana's trademark singing lead tone but also a clean, rotating speaker sound used in the second melodic section.

The track starts with a C minor based melody which contrasts long held notes with short staccato ones, by now a trademark of Santana's playing style. There are times when his guitar seems to be taking a breath during or between phrases – showing the influence of singers on his playing – as he tries to emulate the emotional potential and expressive range of the human voice.

The solo is played over a two chord 'vamp'. This creates a broad backdrop for Santana to play over – and he takes full advantage.

Tablature Key

Hammer-on

Play the first note with one finger then 'hammer' another finger on the fret indicated.

Pull-off

Place both fingers on the notes to be sounded, play the first note and, without picking, pull the finger off to sound the lower note.

Gliss

Play the first note and then slide the same fret-hand finger up or down to the second note. Don't strike the second note.

Gliss and restrike

Same as legato slide, except the second note is struck.

Quarter-tone bend

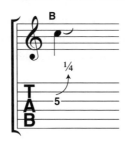

Play the note then bend up a quarter-tone.

Half-tone bend

Play the note then bend up a semi-tone.

Whole-tone bend

Play the note then bend up a whole-tone.

Bend of more than a tone

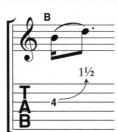

Play the note then bend up as required.

Bend and return

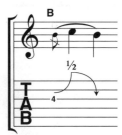

Play the note, bend up as indicated, then return back to the original note.

Compound bend and return

Play the note then bend up and down in the rhythm shown.

Pre-bend

Bend the note as shown before striking.

Pre-bend and return

Bend the note as shown before striking it, then return it back to its original pitch.

Unison bend

Play the two notes together and bend the lower note up to the pitch of the higher one.

Double stop bend and return

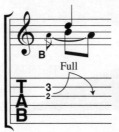

Hold the top note, then bend and return the bottom notes on a lower string.

Bend and restrike

Play the note, bend as shown, then restrike the string where indicated.

Bend and tap

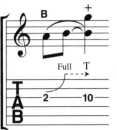

Bend the note as shown and tap the higher fret while still holding the bend.

Vibrato

Rapidly bend and release the note with the fretting hand.

Trill

Rapidly alternate between the notes indicated by continuously hammering on and pulling off.

Tapping

Hammer ('tap') the fret indicated with the pick-hand index or middle finger and pull off the note fretted by the fret-hand.

Pick scrape

The edge of the pick is rubbed along the string, producing a scratchy sound.

Muffled strings

Lay the fret-hand lightly across the strings then play with the pick-hand.

Natural harmonic

Play the note while the fret-hand lightly touches the string directly over the fret indicated.

Pinch harmonic

Fret the note normally and produce a harmonic by adding the edge of the thumb or the tip of the index finger of the pick hand to the normal pick attack.

Harp harmonic

Fret the note normally and gently rest the pick-hand's index finger directly above the indicated fret while the pick-hand's thumb or pick assists by plucking the appropriate string.

Palm muting

Allow the pick-hand to rest lightly on the strings whilst playing.

Rake

Drag the pick across the strings shown with a single motion.

Tremolo picking

Repeatedly pick the note as rapidly as possible.

Arpeggiate

Play the notes of the chord by rolling them in the direction of the arrow.

Vibrato-bar dive and return

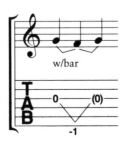

Drop the pitch of the note or chord a specific number of steps (in rhythm) then return to the original pitch.

Vibrato-bar dips

Play the first note then use the bar to drop a specific number of steps, then release back to the original pitch, in rhythm. Only the first note is picked.

FLOR D'LUNA

by Tom Coster

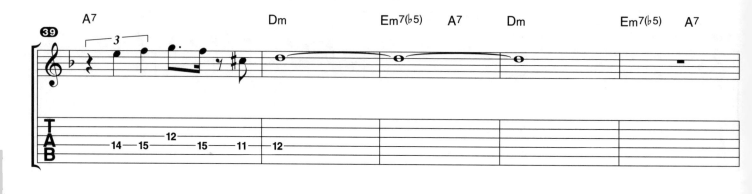

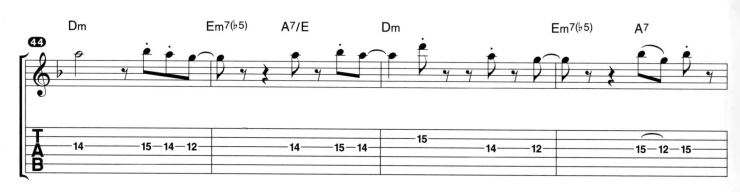

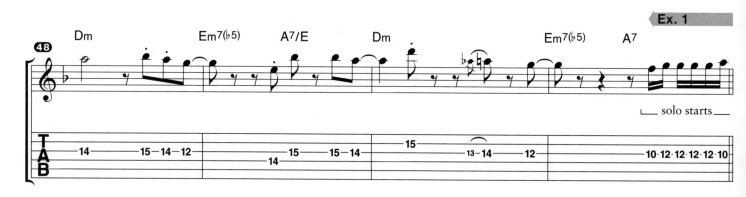

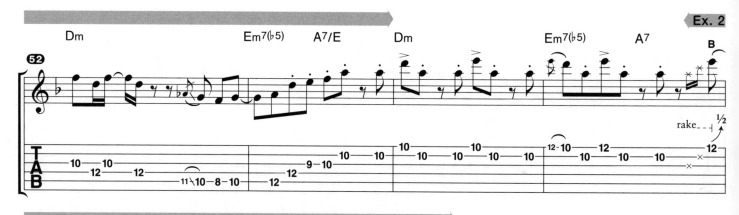

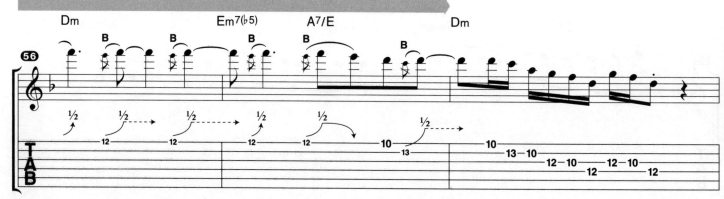

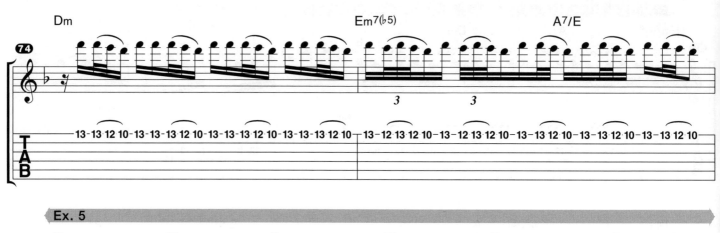

Ex. 5

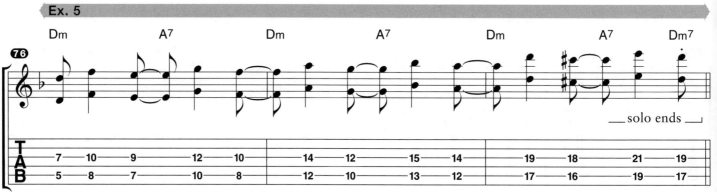

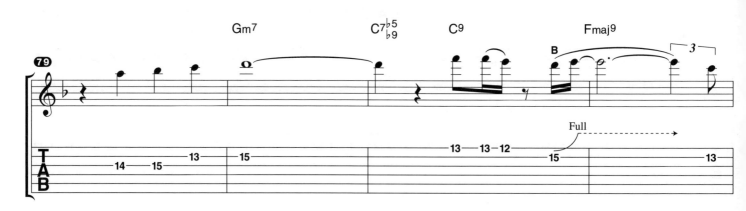

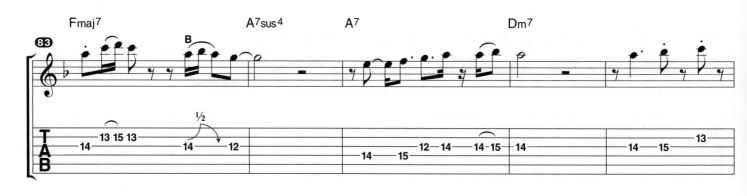

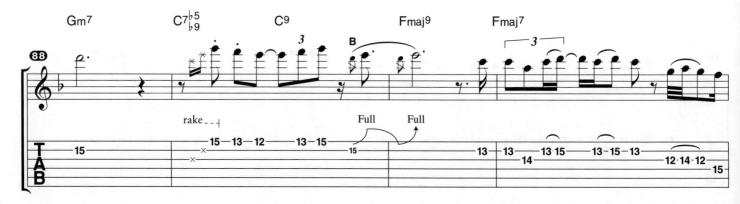

The Solo

Flor D' Luna

What a great way to announce the start of your solo! A machine-gun burst of fast picking in the 10th fret D minor pentatonic position contrasts dramatically with the sparse and measured melody that goes before it. This clearly announces the start of the solo to the listener, even though the backing continues pretty much as before. After this dynamic opening phrase Carlos eases back on the throttle, and allows the solo to settle into a more laid back feel.

Ex 1

Santana's solos all have a feeling of progression to them, a sense of increasing tension. Just one of the many techniques he employs to create this effect is a repeated and syncopated string bend. Let's take a look at one.

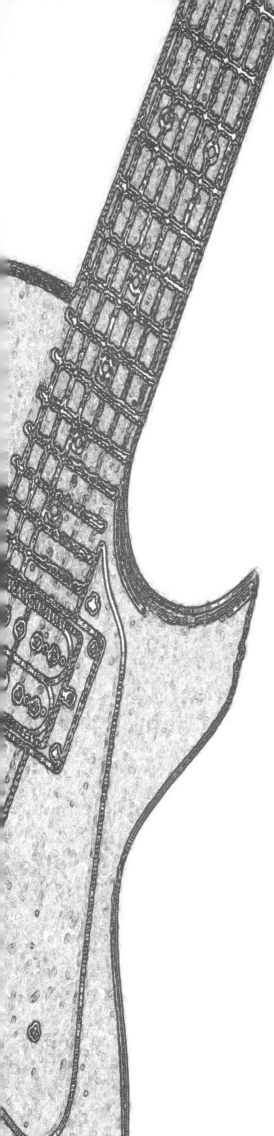

Ex 2

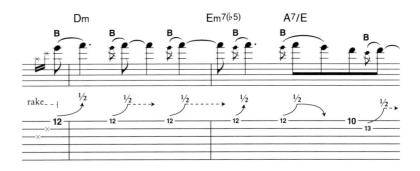

This example is taken from early in the solo, so the bend is in a fairly low register and he's bending only half a tone, but you definitely get the feeling of momentum building up. For this phrase you should be in the 10th position, so your first finger is on the 10th fret. The string bends should be played with the third finger and, as with any bends, supported by the first and second.

Ex 3

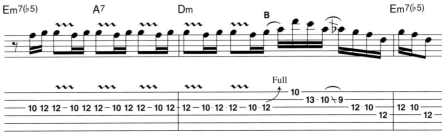

Here's another use of repetition. Note the vibrato on the G note. Santana uses very little vibrato and when he does it's subtle and used to good effect. In the second bar is a bluesy descending run. Unusually, the Ab on beat three is played on the B string. Most players would play this on the G string but not Carlos – he uses a first finger slide to slip that chromatic passing note in.

In bars 61-63 we see further use of syncopated string bends, this time full bends that lead up to the high point of the solo where we see a great example of Carlos' nimble finger work.

The first position shift here is played with the third finger. Then, during the rest, move back to the 10th fret position for the triplet pull-off phrase.

Ex4

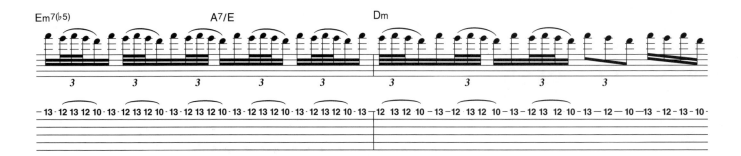

This is the hardest part of the solo so it may need some work. Use your third finger for the F and second for the E, with your first finger covering the 10th fret. The sheer number of notes can be daunting but it's far simpler than it looks.

What we have here is a repeating pattern played in a cross rhythm. If you learn the first four notes of this bar you've got the whole thing. Play through the phrase slowly and

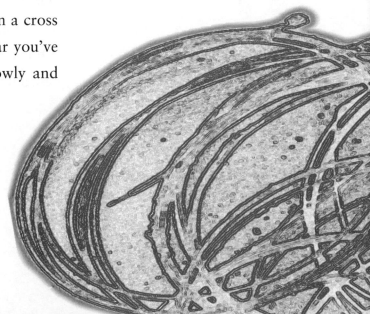

learn which notes land on the strong beats, then gradually speed it up.

The soaring high register melody starting in bar 69 is immediately followed by a another fast legato phrase. Treat this one in the same way as the previous one. The solo ends with an ascending octave phrase.

Ex 5

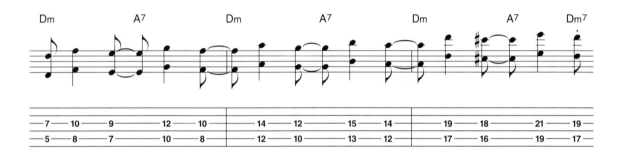

The sound for this lick is cleaner, almost jazzy, and was probably played by using the neck pickup and by strumming the strings with the thumb. Use your first and third fingers to play the octave shape. The whole phrase is on the same pair of strings, so to make life easier concentrate on just the bottom note, and the top one will follow along.

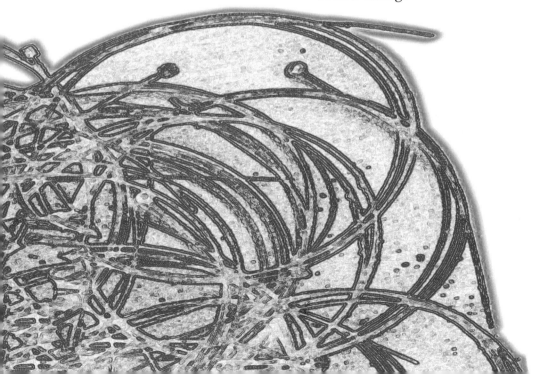

ALL I EVER WANTED

Words and Music by Carlos Santana, Chris Solberg and Alex Ligertwood

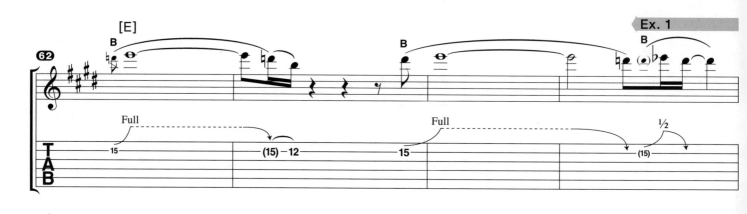

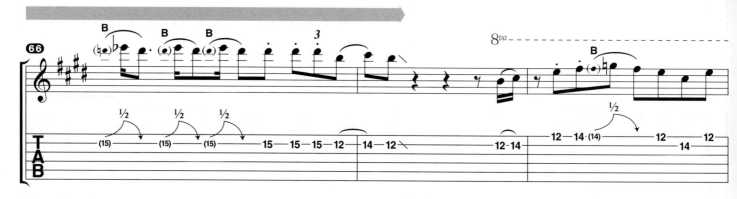

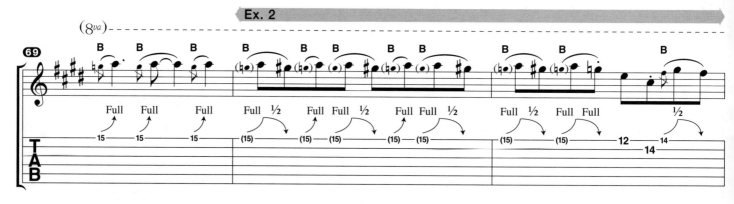

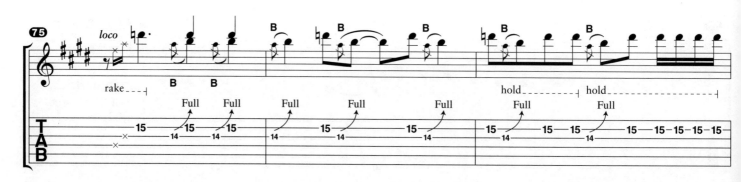

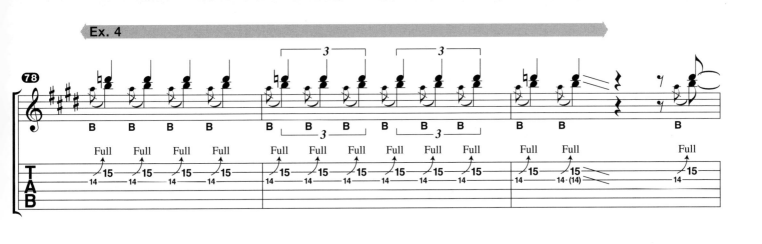

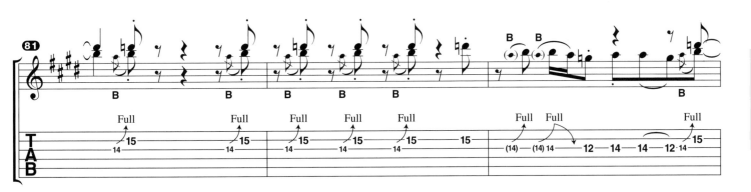

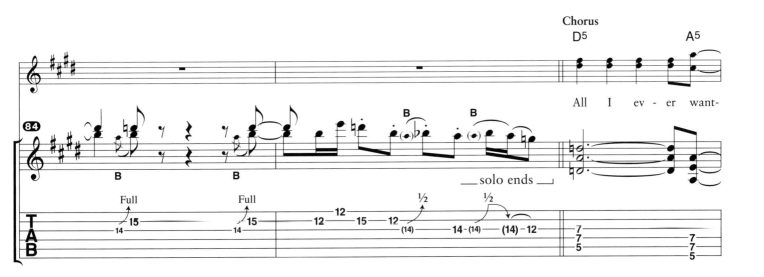

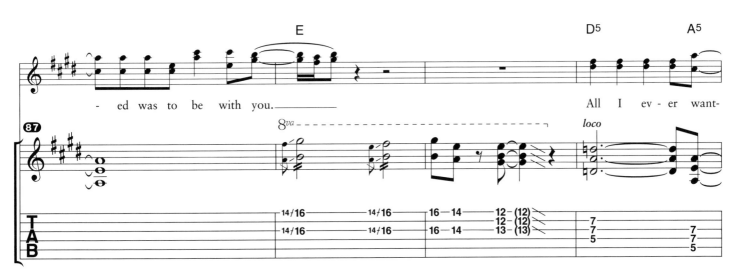

All I Ever Wanted   **25**

The Solo

All I Ever Wanted

In a fast and busy track like this there is a great deal of truth in the old saying 'less is more'. The strong opening phrase in bar 61 is a good example of how to make the most of a simple idea. The first few notes feature a combination of a unison bend and a re-bend. This involves bending the B string with the third finger, releasing and re-bending it whilst the top note is held on the E string with your first finger.

Ex1

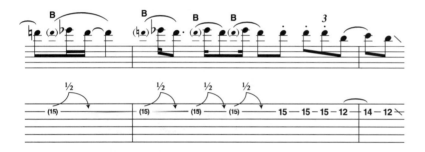

The half tone pre-bends in these two bars are very short, with the E♮ acting almost as a grace note to the repeated D.

Ex2

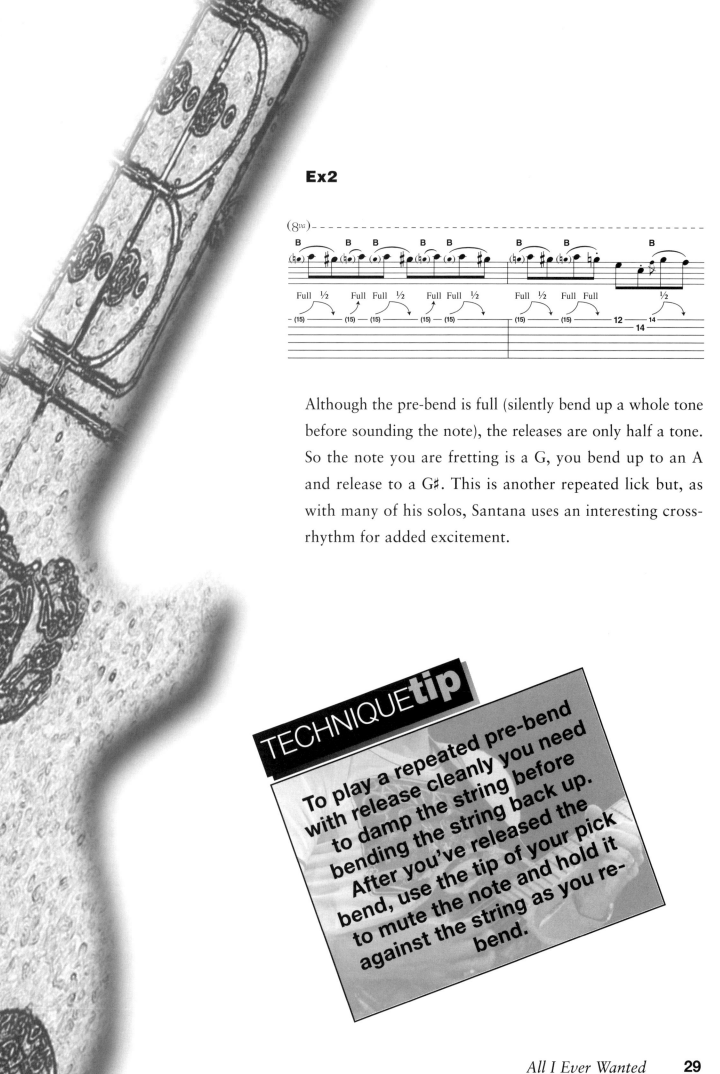

Although the pre-bend is full (silently bend up a whole tone before sounding the note), the releases are only half a tone. So the note you are fretting is a G, you bend up to an A and release to a G♯. This is another repeated lick but, as with many of his solos, Santana uses an interesting cross-rhythm for added excitement.

TECHNIQUEtip

To play a repeated pre-bend with release cleanly you need to damp the string before bending the string back up. After you've released the bend, use the tip of your pick to mute the note and hold it against the string as you re-bend.

You'll need to concentrate on the pitch of the bends here. Not just the pre-bend note but also the release note. To add extra spice you can make this note a little "sharp" by not releasing it all the way.

Ex3

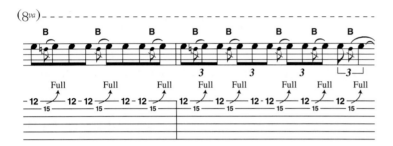

This whole solo is constructed around simple, repetitive ideas but the repeated phrases are never exactly the same twice. In this bending lick Carlos breaks into a triplet rhythm to give a sense of acceleration.

The rest of the solo is based around a double stop and string bend. The D note is held on the B string with the first finger while you use your third finger to bend the G string.

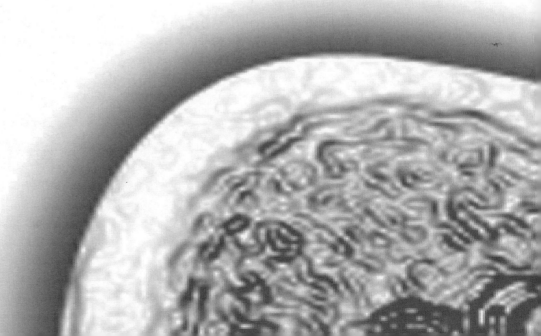

Ex 4

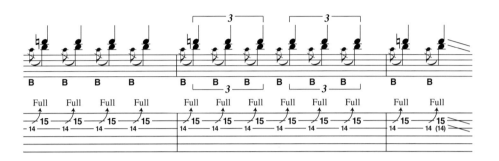

Notice how Carlos introduces this idea in bars 76-77 before hitting you with it full-on. After a bar he again uses the triplet rhythm to build the lick. Make sure the finger that's holding down the top note is relaxed while your third finger bends the G string.

This bend is used in a variety of rhythmic patterns to the end of the solo.

SENSITIVE KIND

Words and Music by J J Cale

The Solo

Sensitive Kind

The solo on this song is a model of taste and restraint. Sure, it's impressive to burn around the fingerboard, and the high energy approach certainly has its merits, but so too does the understated, cool style we see here. Notice how Carlos isn't afraid to leave space in his solo. Indeed there is a well-known saying in jazz – it's not what you play that counts, it's what you don't play!

Ex 1

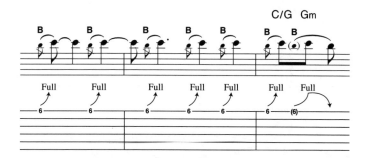

The syncopated string bend lick in bar 31 is low down the neck in the G minor position on the third fret. This makes it harder to bend the string, so use your third finger to play the note and use fingers one and two behind it, so you are pushing the string with all three. Pick the strings close to the bridge to get close to the original tone.

This is yet another example of Santana using a Latin influenced cross rhythm to create tension in his solo.

Most of the action takes place at either the 3rd fret or 15th fret G minor positions, with a few phrases played around the 11th fret.

Ex 2

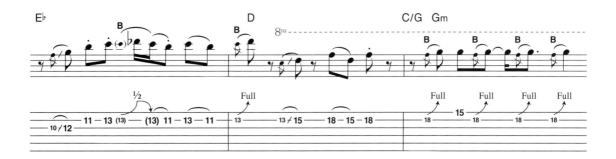

If you use your second finger to slide into the G, your third finger will automatically be set up to play the bends on the B string. The position shift should be incorporated smoothly into the musical phrase. Using the first finger, slide from the C to D note on the B string. You are now in the 15th G minor position, essential for the string bends in the third bar of the example.

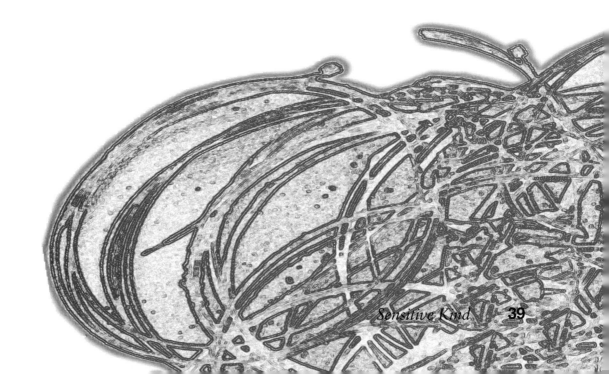

Ex 3

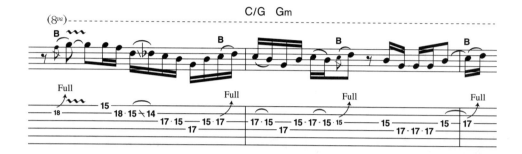

In this example Santana uses a first finger slide to play the Db note on the B string. This phrase is more commonly played with that note on the G string, but playing it this way gives a more fluid sound to the lick. You'll need to keep your fretting hand relaxed for this phrase – it's quite fast and you need to play it smoothly for it to work. Once again use your third finger to bend the G string. At the end of the example you need to hammer-on from the Bb to the C before bending the C up to D.

We're back in the third position for the next phrase, combining pre-bends with staccato notes. These staccato notes are an important part of Santana's style, as they occur throughout his music, and add great energy to even the simplest lines.

TECHNIQUEtip

In the fourth bar there is another smooth position change. This gear change is so slick because the first note of the new phrase is the same as the last note of the previous one. You can use this technique to break out of the 'blues box' playing and increase the range of your licks.

Ex 4

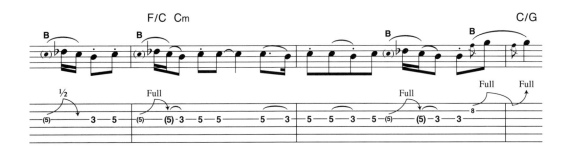

Notice in the second full bar of the example that there is a pull-off from C to B♭, and the B♭ is marked with a staccato dot. Use your picking hand to damp the string instead of just lifting off with your fretting hand.

Ex 5

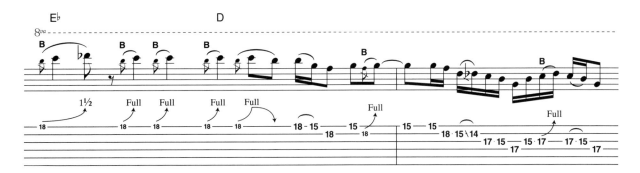

For the last phrase we've moved up to the 15th position again, starting with a 1½ tone bend from B♭ to D♭ on the top string. Remember to support your third finger for extra strength in the string bends.

SAMBA PA TI

by Carlos Santana

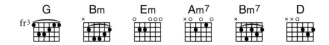

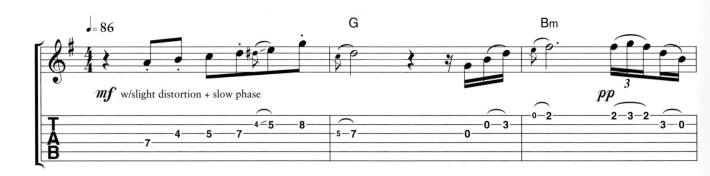

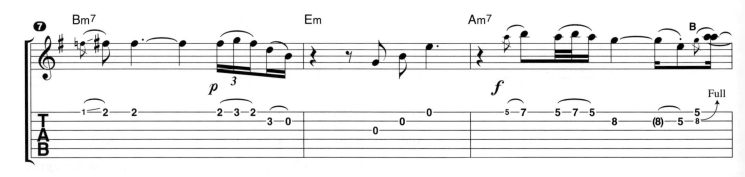

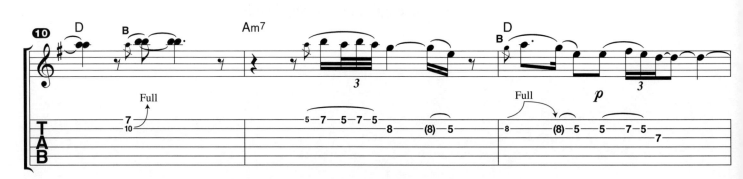

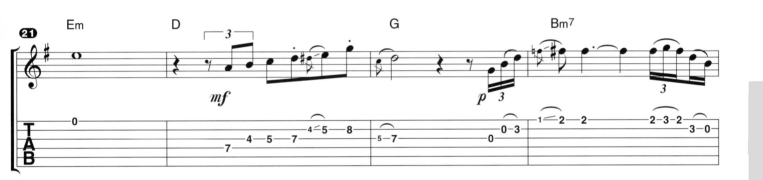

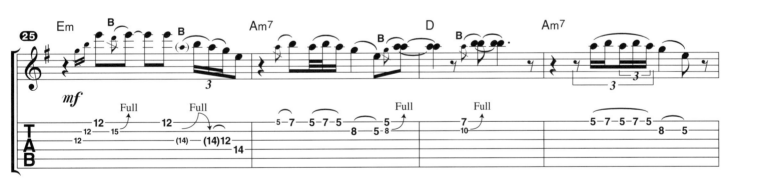

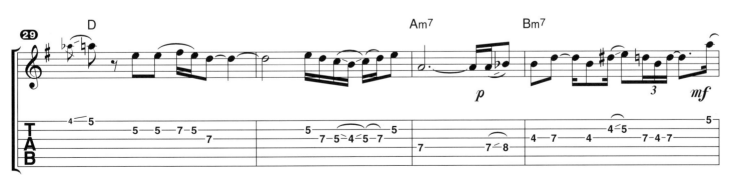

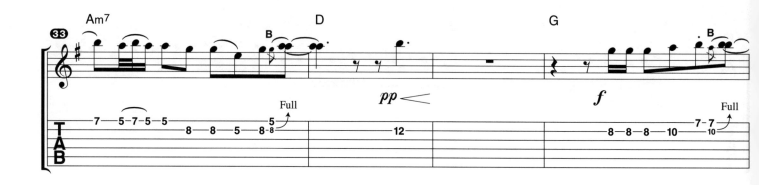

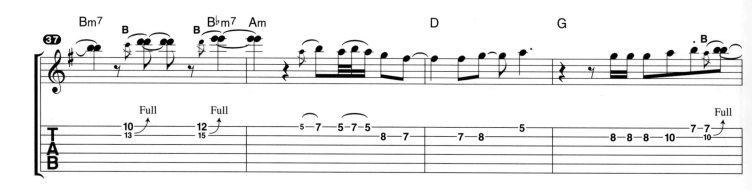

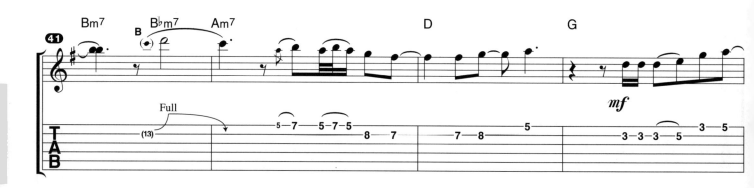

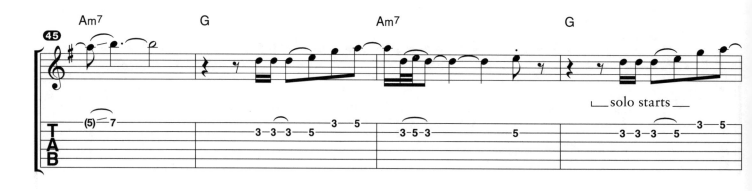

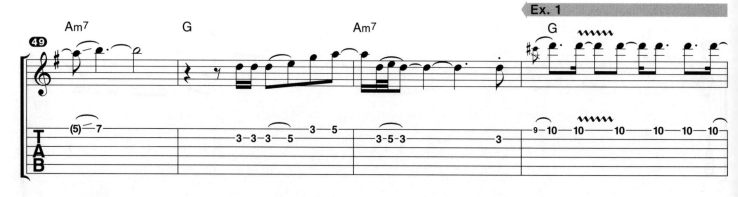

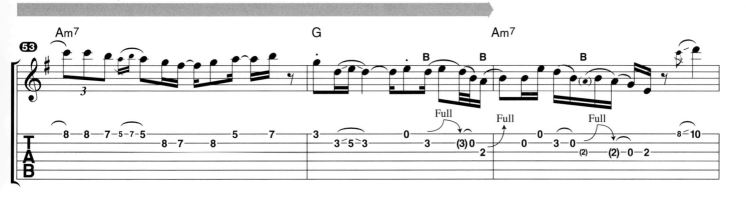

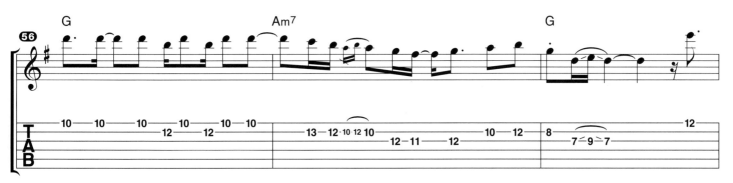

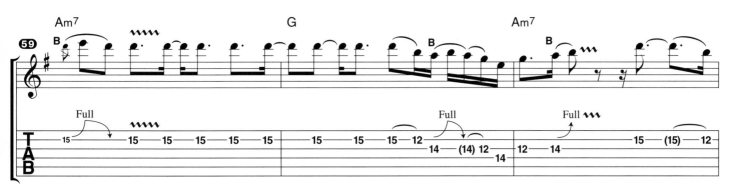

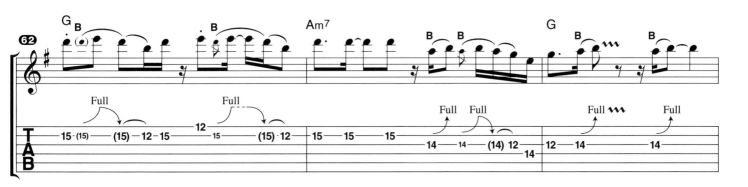

Ex. 2

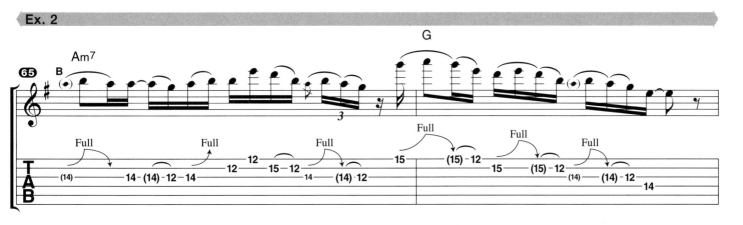

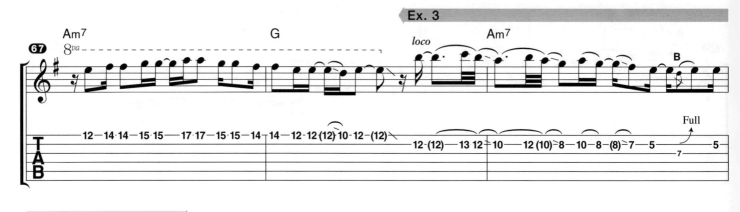

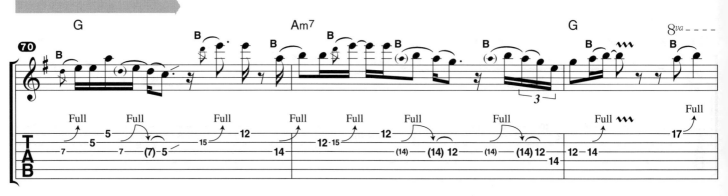

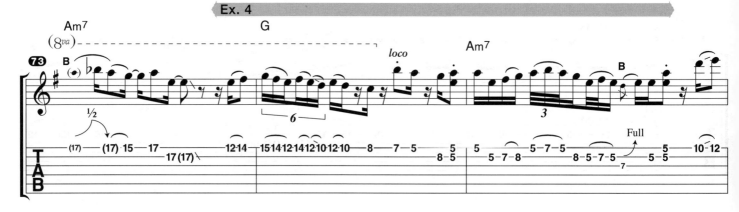

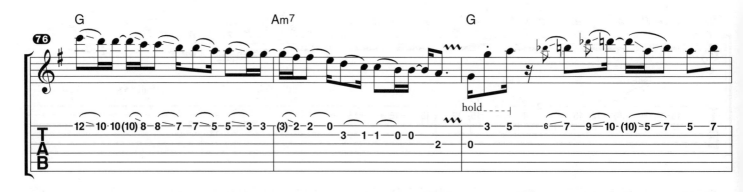

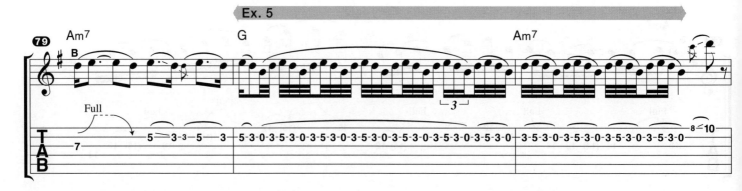

The Solo

Samba Pa Ti

This song is the key of G and starts around the 3rd fret but incorporates a lot of position changes. As Santana is primarily a melodic guitarist these position shifts are used to emphasise the phrasing of the melody. He combines this with a very effective use of dynamics, usually achieved by adjusting his guitar's volume control between phrases. These small touches are almost as important as the notes themselves, as they really breathe life into the music.

The opening melodic phrase takes off into a syncopated repeated D note.

Ex 1

This phrase spans four positions so we need to look at the shifts in detail to make them smooth. Use your third finger for the slide and vibrato. In the second bar of the example you need to make a rapid position shift to the 5th fret. You do this playing both the D at the end of the first bar and the C in the second with your third finger. This sets up your

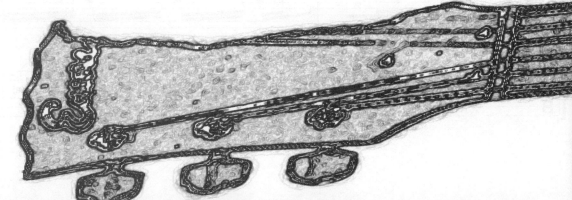

This fast legato lick is played with fingers one and three. Because the movement of your fretting hand may cause you to hit the other strings you'll need to use your picking hand to damp the strings on either side of the one you are playing.

hand for the hammer-on in the next beat. In the 3rd bar play the G and the B string slide with your first finger. After the open E string play the B string bend with your second finger to move you into the open E minor position.

This long outro solo is played over a two chord vamp of G and Am7. It's mostly played from this point on around the 12th fret which works well for both these chords.

Ex 2

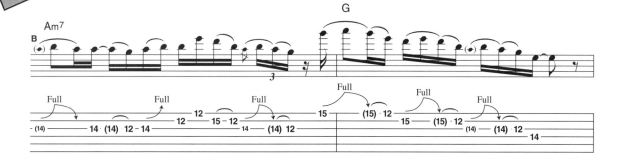

Most of the bends in this example are played long, especially in the 2nd bar where the flow of the lick shouldn't be interrupted by the bent notes. Use normal pentatonic fingering here with the first finger barring the first two strings.

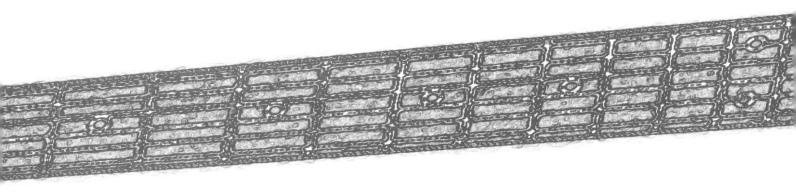

Ex 3

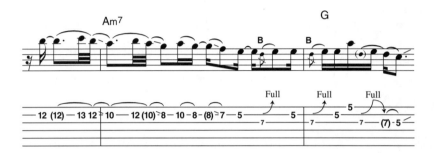

This is a tricky phrase to play as it combines hammer-ons and pull-offs with slides and position shifts. Starting with your first finger, in a smooth motion, hammer-on and pull-off with your second finger then slide down with the first finger. Next do the same but this time with the third finger hammering-on.

Ex 4

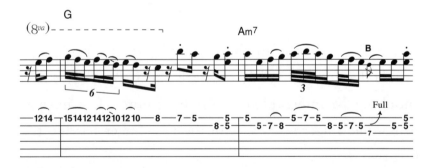

This example sees us back at the 12th fret for a quick legato phrase. Again you have to do a first finger slide after the pull-offs. Use the rest in beat 2 to move your hand so that you can play the C with your third finger. This moves you into the 4th fret A minor position for the legato phrases in the second bar.

The slides in the following bars (76 and 77) can all be played with your second finger.

Ex 5

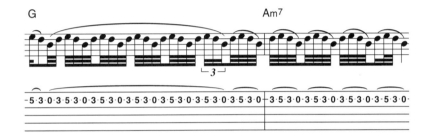

Although this is another scary-looking phrase don't be put off by the sheer quantity of notes. There are really only three different notes here, all played on the B string so, once you have this short lick under your fingers, you just need to repeat it.

Notice that in the first bar almost all notes are slurred. This changes in the second bar where Carlos picks the first note of each four-note group.

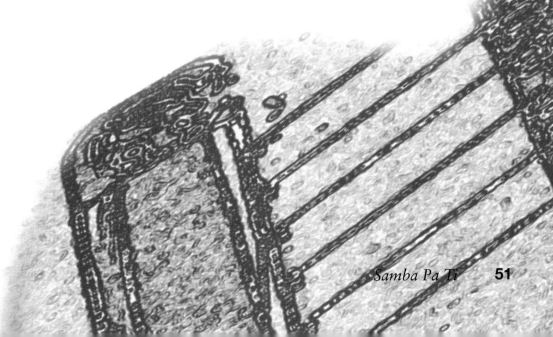

EUROPA

by Carlos Santana and Tom Coster

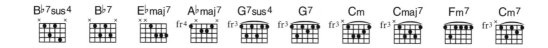

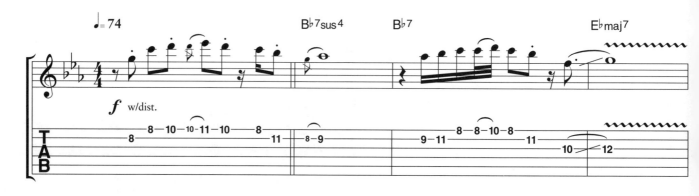

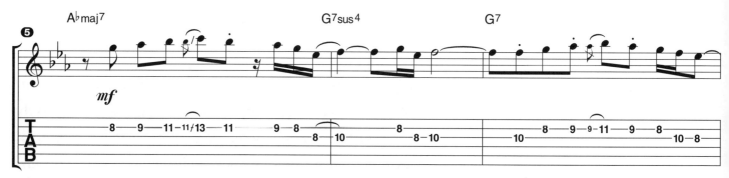

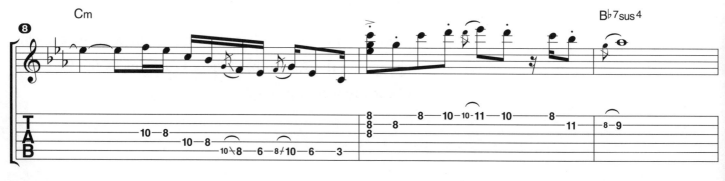

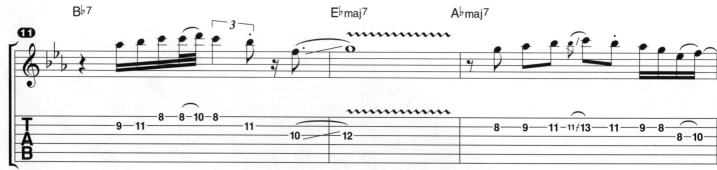

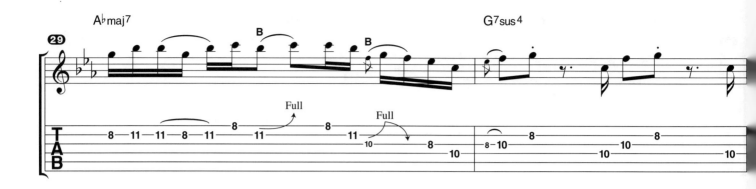

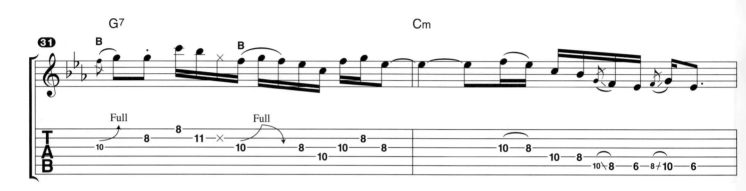

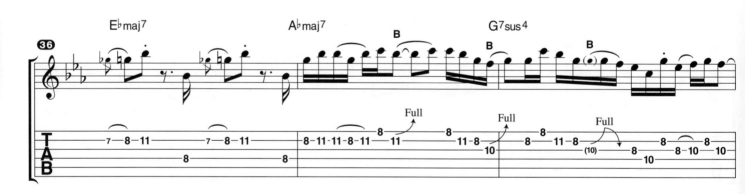

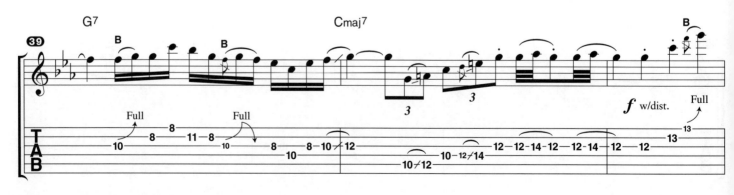

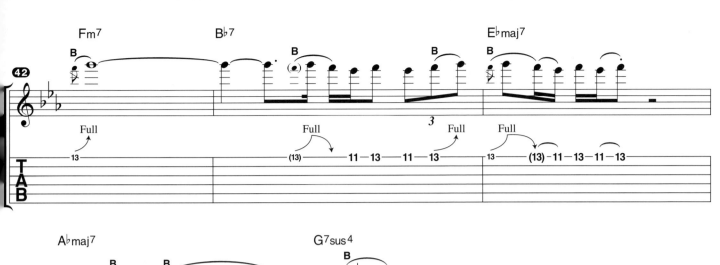

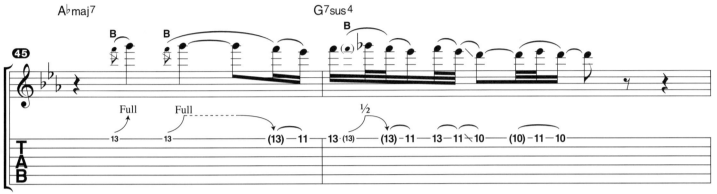

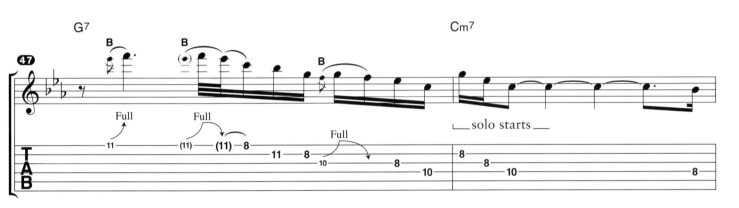

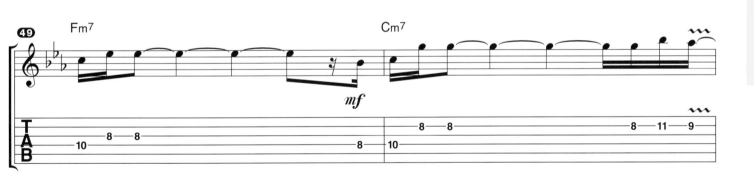

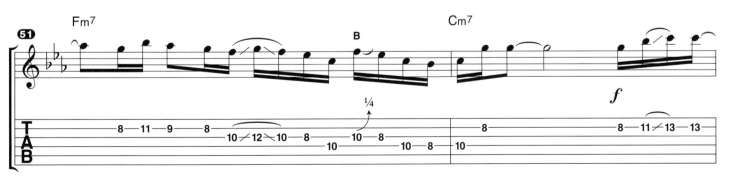

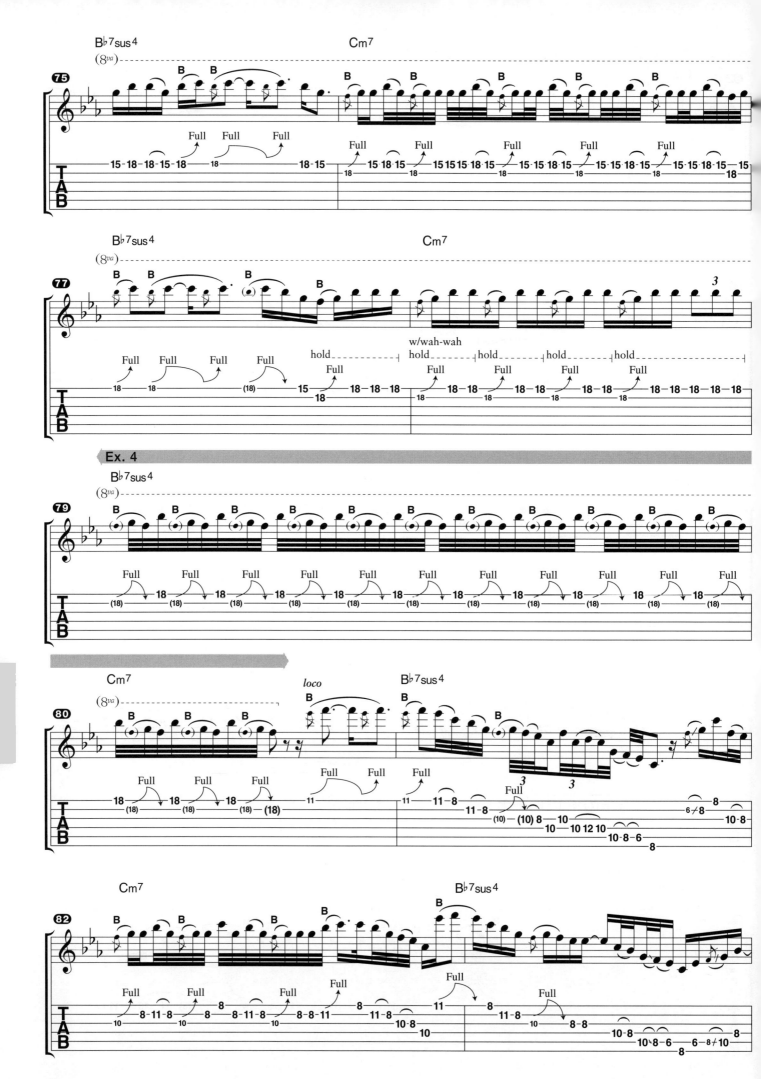

The Solo

Europa

This solo is a good example of Carlos' trademark 'singing' guitar style which builds from sparsely used simple lines into some intense and expressive guitar playing. All of Carlos' favourite moves are here from lightning fast flurries of notes to long, sustained string bends.

This solo is played over Fm7 and Cm7 and stays mostly around the 8th fret C minor position.

Ex 1

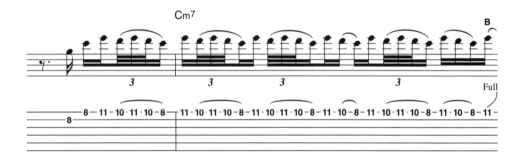

To learn this lick you're going to need to slow it down and learn the finger moves thoroughly. If you think of the fast triplet as one smooth movement from the second finger D note through E♭ to the C it will help you get up to speed. Once you've learned the notes you'll see the four note pattern clearly. It looks more complicated on paper because of the way it falls across the beat.

Santana really raids his box of tricks for this solo, and many of his classic techniques are on view, like the syncopated, repeating notes in bars 57 and 60.

Even in the middle of a passionate solo Carlos finds room for a memorable tune.

Ex 2

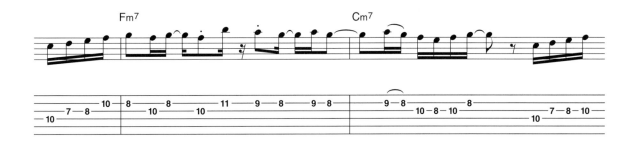

Use scale fingering for this example, starting with your fourth finger. Emphasise the contrast between the held notes and the short, staccato notes. Only by using this kind of phrasing can you really bring a melody to life in the way that Carlos does.

After this brief melodic interlude we head back into more improvisational territory.

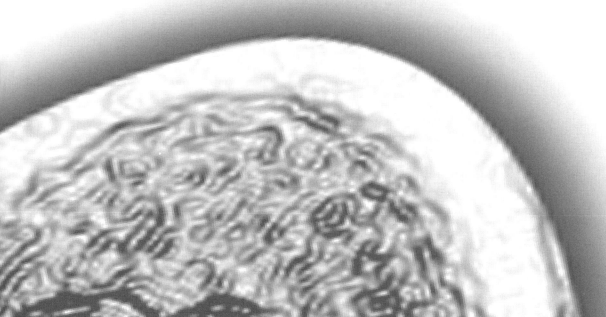

Ex 3

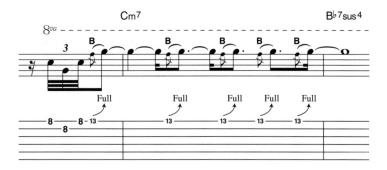

Think of the three notes before the bend in this example as grace notes. Play the F with your third finger and really milk those string bends!

Ex 4

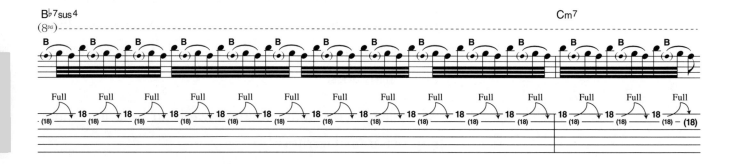

This three note repeating pattern starts with a pre-bend before releasing with a B♭ played on the top string. Use the fourth finger on the top string and don't be afraid to let it ring as you play the B string bends. The tricky part here is getting the speed and rhythm right. Once again the slower you practice it the faster you'll learn it.

Photo: Richard Aaron

TECHNIQUE*tip*

To achieve the kind of endless sustain that Carlos uses you'll need to move around, while you play, until you find the 'sweet spot'. This is usually directly in line with your amp. If you turn down the guitar's tone control and don't use too much distortion or vibrato you should feel a direct connection between your guitar and amplifier and your notes will sing like Santana's!

HANNIBAL

Words and Music by Carlos Santana, Raul Rekow, Alex Ligertwood and Alan Pasqua

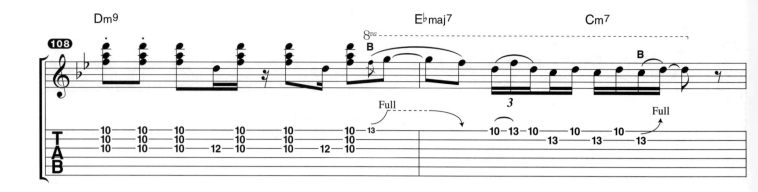

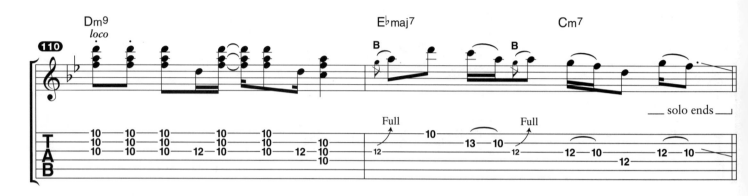

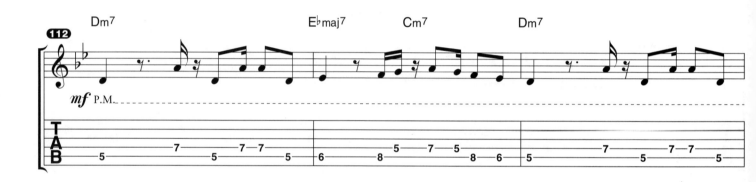

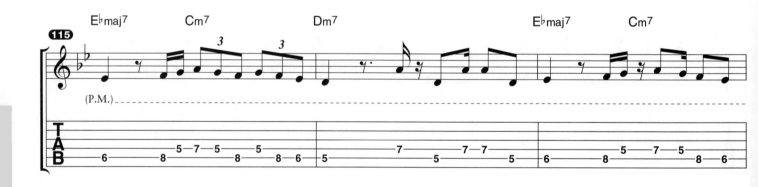

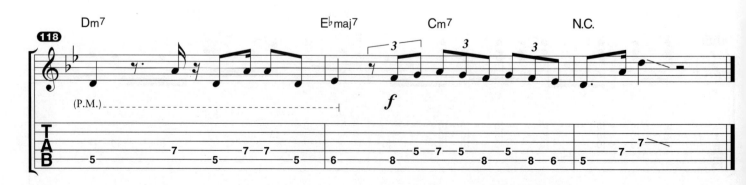

The Solo

Hannibal

This is a great high energy solo that blisters into action with a fast ascending scale that soars to a repeated F on the top string.

Ex 1

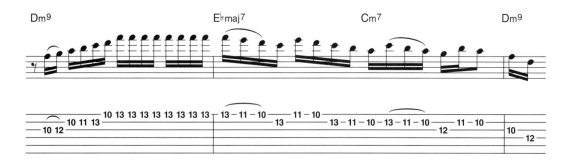

Play this in the 10th fret position, and use scale fingering so that the top note is played by the fourth finger. The fingering is important here because you need to set up the pull-offs that happen on the way down. Santana uses a lot of fast repeated picking (or tremolo picking). He plays with a large triangular pick that comes to a sharp point and, when he's playing this kind of phrase, he'll pick close to the bridge. This helps him achieve the fast picking speed required for this lick.

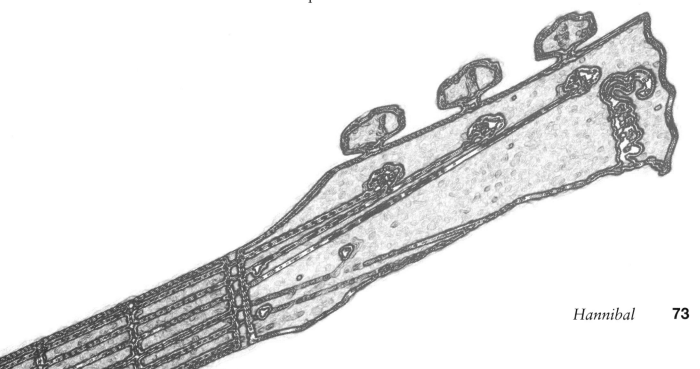

Ex2

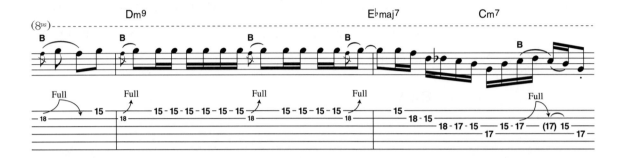

After a quick position change up to the 15th fret Santana keeps the excitement going with a phrase made up of fast string bends and repeated notes. Don't hold the bend when you play the top note this time, and when you get to the fast descending pentatonic line try and pick each of the notes.

In bars 68 and 69 notice the phrasing of the two note groups. The second note is always staccato and plays with the rhythmic emphasis, which gives a great sense of movement up to the bend in bar 69.

Ex 3

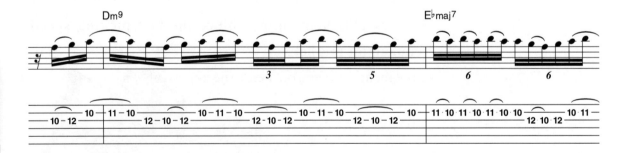

This is a repeated four note pattern that seems to gradually speed up until the first beat of the second bar, where the pattern changes. The rhythm is quicker here too, with the overall impression being of an acceleration. To help you learn this lick, break it down into smaller chunks, say, one beat at a time. Learn each phrase slowly then piece them together.

The high point of the whole solo is a long repeating pre-bend lick which appears in bars 86 – 88.

Ex 4

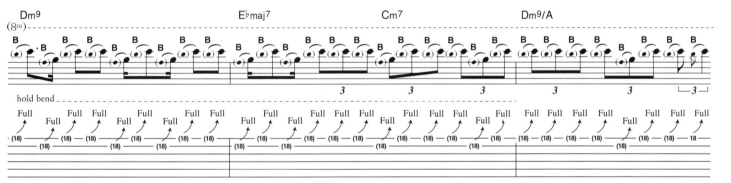

This phrase involves playing pre-bends in close succession on two different strings. There's no time to bend each string separately so you have to bend both strings in one movement. When you bend the top string make sure that you catch the B string, and bend that by the same amount but without sounding it. Now hold the bend on both strings and play the notes. The problem you have is to stop the string ringing after you have played it. You can't use your fretting hand to damp the string because it's busy, so you have to simultaneously pick the note and, with the pick, damp the previous one. This isn't as hard as it sounds and, once you've got the hang of it, you should be able to recreate the original very closely.

In the final bars of the solo Carlos alternates a syncopated three-note chord with bluesy pentatonic lines.

Ex 5

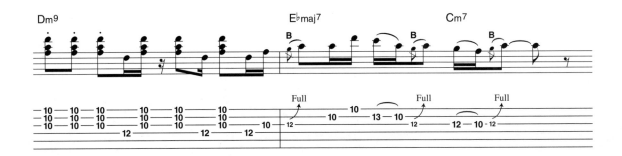

To play the chord, barre the top three strings with your first finger. Make sure you lift off on the staccato chords. For the pentatonic licks use your third finger to bend the G string, and a first finger barre at the 10th fret. You can use either your third or fourth finger to play the pull-offs on the B string, whichever you are most comfortable with.